BOUNCING BACK FROM EXTINCTION

THE RETURN OF THE
GRAY WOLF

CAITIE MCANENEY

PowerKiDS press.
New York

Published in 2018 by The Rosen Publishing Group, Inc.
29 East 21st Street, New York, NY 10010

First Edition

Editor: Theresa Morlock
Book Design: Reann Nye

Photo Credits: Cover, p. 28 Geoffrey Kuchera/Shutterstock.com; p. 4 Bildagentur Zoonar GmbH/Shutterstock.com; p. 5 (Pyrenean ibex) dragoms/Moment Open/Getty Images; p. 5 (jaguar) Travel Stock/Shutterstock.com; p. 5 (Arctic fox, hippopotamus) bikeriderlondon/Shutterstock.com; p. 5 (orangutan) Sergey Uryadnikov/Shutterstock.com; p. 5 (Wyoming toad) https://commons.wikimedia.org/wiki/File:Bufo_baxteri-3.jpg; p. 7 Naturfoto Honal/Corbis Documentary/Getty Images; p. 8 Ronnie Howard/Shutterstock.com; p. 9 kochanowski/Shutterstock.com; p. 10 tony mills/Shutterstock.com; p. 11 avs/Shutterstock.com; p. 12 (grizzly bear) ashleykirkpatrick/Shutterstock.com; p. 12 (fox) RT Images/Shutterstock.com; p. 13 Frank Pali/All Canada Photos/Getty Images; p. 15 Underwood Archives/Archive Photos/Getty Images; p. 16 (manatee) Greg Amptman/Shutterstock.com; p. 16 (bald eagle) FloridaStock/Shutterstock.com; p. 16 (American bison) AndreAnita/Shutterstock.com; p. 17 Holly Kuchera/Shutterstock.com; p. 18 William F. Campbell/The LIFE Images Collection/Getty Images; pp. 19, 21 William Campbell/Sygma/Getty Images; pp. 22, 29 critterbiz/Shutterstock.com; p. 23 1tomm/Shutterstock.com; p. 24 Dennis W Donohue/Shutterstock.com; p. 25 Donald M. Jones/Minden Pictures/Getty Images; p. 27 Daniel J. Cox/Corbis Documentary/Getty Images; p. 30 Thomas Barrat/Shutterstock.com.

Cataloging-in-Publication Data

Names: McAneney, Caitie.
Title: The return of the gray wolf / Caitie McAneney.
Description: New York : PowerKids Press, 2018. | Series: Bouncing Back from Extinction | Includes index.
Identifiers: ISBN 9781508156253 (pbk.) | ISBN 9781508156185 (library bound) | ISBN 9781508156062 (6 pack)
Subjects: LCSH: Gray wolf–North America–Juvenile literature.
Classification: LCC QL737.C22 M367 2018 | DDC 599.773–dc23

Manufactured in the United States of America

CPSIA Compliance Information: Batch #BS17PK: For Further Information contact Rosen Publishing, New York, New York at 1-800-237-9932

THE GREAT GRAY WOLF

The gray wolf is one of the most **fascinating** creatures in North America. As a large and fearsome predator, the gray wolf should be the ruler of its natural **ecosystem**. However, because of its difficult history with people, this wolf was once pushed to the brink of extinction in the United States.

For thousands of years, native peoples in North America lived with respect for the gray wolf. They created stories and legends about this howling hunter. Some worshipped the wolf and believed it to be a creature of great spiritual power. However, when European settlers came to North America, they considered the gray wolf a threat. Settlers harmed the gray wolf's ecosystem and made it their mission to wipe out the gray wolf population for good.

The gray wolf's return from near extinction is one of the most amazing comebacks in natural history.

CONSERVATION STATUS CHART

EXTINCT

Having no living members.

Pyrenean ibex

EXTINCT IN THE WILD

Living members only in captivity.

Wyoming toad

CRITICALLY ENDANGERED

At highest risk of becoming extinct.

Sumatran orangutan

ENDANGERED VULNERABLE

High risk of extinction in the wild.

hippopotamus

NEAR THREATENED

Likely to become endangered soon.

jaguar

LEAST CONCERN

Lowest risk of endangerment.

Arctic fox

MEET THE GRAY WOLF

Gray wolves are the largest of all species, or kinds, of wolves. They're also the largest members of the canine, or dog, family. Scientists believe the dogs we keep as pets today **descended** from wolves many thousands of years ago.

Gray wolves are often gray, as their name suggests. They also have a mix of black, white, or brown hair, and their color often depends on the area in which they live. Their fur color can help them blend in with their surroundings when following prey.

Gray wolves are known for their nighttime howls. That sound has become part of many scary stories. In reality, the wolves are just communicating with one another. They have close families, and every wolf has a part in hunting and protecting the pack.

WOLF PACK BONDS

Wolf packs are usually very close family units. Wolves are very social animals, which means they live and hunt together. Each pack has a social order. The alpha couple is the most powerful male and female of the pack. The members of a pack live together and help raise young. When the wolf pack hunts, each member has a certain job. They cooperate, or work together, to plan and carry out the attack.

A wolf pack often has between six and 10 wolves in it. Bigger packs can take down bigger animals when they hunt.

WHEN WOLVES ROAMED THE LAND

Before European settlers arrived, gray wolves hunted and lived as they pleased, had few threats to their safety, and were found all over the Northern **Hemisphere**. They lived from Canada to Mexico, including in today's United States, and in parts of Europe and Asia. Wolves are very adaptable creatures, which means they change to live better in their surroundings.

WOLVES IN NATIVE AMERICAN CULTURE

The Hopi, Quileute, Arikara, and Ojibwe cultures traditionally respect wolves and see them as powerful, spiritual beings. Some Native American nations are involved in efforts to restore wolf populations. In the 1990s the Nez Perce tribe celebrated the return of the wolves to Idaho, holding a ceremony to honor their release into the wild. The White Mountain Apaches of Arizona work closely with other groups to help restore wolves in Mexico.

Gray wolves are the apex, or top, predators in their ecosystems.

They can live in very cold areas, very warm areas, and areas that are in between.

Wolves hunt hoofed animals such as elk, bison, and deer. They also hunt smaller animals such as fish, birds, and snakes. Many native peoples believed that it was wrong to kill wolves, so wolf populations were not at risk.

SETTLERS VS. WOLVES

When European settlers came to North America, they found many groups of Native Americans living off the land. Native peoples lived very peacefully with nature. Europeans had other ways of providing for themselves.

Native Americans usually didn't keep animals. Instead, they hunted wild game. Settlers brought livestock such as cattle, pigs, horses, and sheep. The

Although settlers were afraid of being attacked by wolves, they didn't need to be. In truth, wolves fear people and stay away from them.

WOLVES AND LIVESTOCK

Wolves do not pose a serious threat to livestock. In truth, more livestock are killed by coyotes and pet dogs than by wolves. There are many effective ways of protecting livestock without harming wolves. **Conservationists** encourage farmers and ranchers to use fences and guard dogs to protect their livestock without hurting predators. Wolves tend to be afraid of humans and stay away from people and their homes.

animals mostly ate grass and other plant life around the settlements and were not fenced in. This lack of protection made them targets for wolves. Farmers needed their livestock as sources of food, clothing, and other important resources. Soon, settlers considered the wolf their enemy.

Many settlers were also scared of this predator with its large teeth and yellow eyes. Settlers began to kill wolves out of anger and fear.

SYSTEMATIC KILLING

Some settlers killed wolves by setting traps. These traps used bait to draw wolves close. Some people killed wolves for sport, while others just wanted to keep their livestock safe.

By the late 1800s, the war on wolves had gotten much worse. What started as landowners defending their livestock had turned into **systematic** killing. People were hired to get rid of wolves and were paid for each wolf they killed. Some professional wolf killers hunted wolves with dogs. Others shot them with guns.

fox

grizzly bear

Wolves weren't the only animals that suffered when people used poisoned bait. Other **scavengers** such as foxes and bears also died.

In the late 1870s, people started to poison the dead bodies of animals that wolves often ate. When the wolves ate the poisoned meat, they usually died. This method spread across the United States, and wolf populations dropped greatly.

NEARLY EXTINCT

The U.S. government **sponsored** wolf-killing programs. The U.S. Forest Service worked to get rid of gray wolves living near cattle ranges. The U.S. Bureau of Biological Survey, which had been founded to research wild animals, turned into a bureau committed to wolf extinction.

Settlers and the U.S. government also harmed wolves by killing off bison and other large prey animals in the Southwest. Wolves were starving without their prey. Naturally, they turned to livestock as another food source, which made farmers and ranchers hate them even more.

People continued to hunt the gray wolf until the late 1900s. By that point, these wolves were nearly extinct in the United States. They were wiped out in Yellowstone National Park, which had once been home to a great wolf population. Yellowstone is located mostly in Wyoming with sections in Montana and Idaho.

Wolf hunters earned between $20 and $50 for every wolf they killed. Programs like this lasted until 1965.

RISE OF THE CONSERVATIONISTS

The 1960s and 1970s were a time of great change in the United States. More people began to realize the effects they had on nature and to understand what they could do to help the environment. Wildlife experts educated the public about animals that were endangered, or in danger of dying out, because of human actions.

bald eagle

The American bison, manatee, and bald eagle were also brought back from the brink of extinction because of the Endangered Species Act.

American bison

manatee

On December 28, 1973, President Richard Nixon signed the Endangered Species Act. The act called for the conservation of endangered and threatened species. Under this act, the gray wolf became a protected species. People were no longer allowed to hunt the wolf legally, and a plan was put in place to help the species recover.

WOLVES RETURN TO YELLOWSTONE

The last wolf pack in Yellowstone National Park was killed off in 1926. This greatly impacted the ecosystem of the park. Animals that were once prey for wolves, such as elk, multiplied so much that it was unhealthy for the environment. It was clear that wolves would have to be reintroduced into the park to bring back the natural balance.

DOUG SMITH

Doug Smith (center) is the leader of the Yellowstone Wolf Project. He began work with the project in 1994. Smith started working as a field biologist, but soon ran the whole program. He collected information about wolves by putting radio collars on them. He organized the information and wrote about his findings. Smith still works in Yellowstone National Park with the wolves after more than 20 years of success. His work is a matter of life and death for the gray wolf.

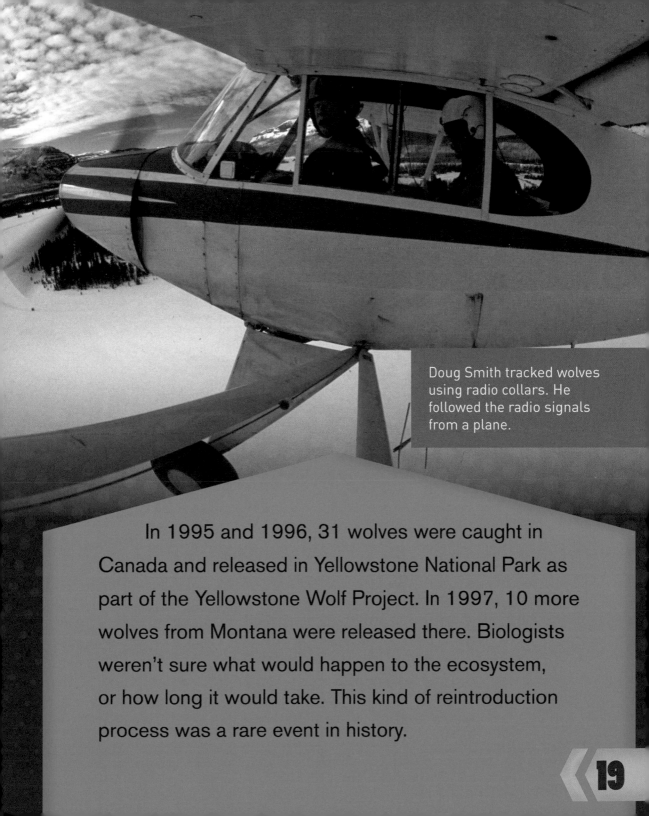

Doug Smith tracked wolves using radio collars. He followed the radio signals from a plane.

In 1995 and 1996, 31 wolves were caught in Canada and released in Yellowstone National Park as part of the Yellowstone Wolf Project. In 1997, 10 more wolves from Montana were released there. Biologists weren't sure what would happen to the ecosystem, or how long it would take. This kind of reintroduction process was a rare event in history.

TRACKING WOLVES

As of 2013, 22 percent of Yellowstone gray wolves had a radio collar. The radio collars help scientists track their movements around the park. Doug Smith and other biologists involved with the Yellowstone Wolf Project had to catch wolves, **tranquilize** them, and put the collars on. What does the information learned through these collars tell us?

Smith and others collect data about the wolves' locations. The collars tell experts about wolf migration, or movement, and hunting styles. The tracking devices also tell biologists about individual wolf behaviors and life in a wolf pack. The more biologists know about wolves in Yellowstone National Park, the more they understand the effect of the wolves on their ecosystem. Smith charted and wrote about his findings, which raised awareness for the Yellowstone Wolf Project.

Doug Smith gets up close to the wolves he studies. Here, he checks a radio collar on this wolf.

A RIPPLE EFFECT

When a stone is dropped into water, it creates ripples, or tiny waves. These ripples spread out farther and farther in all directions. In a similar way, tiny changes like ripples started to happen at Yellowstone National Park.

When the wolves were gone, elk ate plants and trees in the same location all year round. They especially loved eating aspen, cottonwood, and willow trees. They

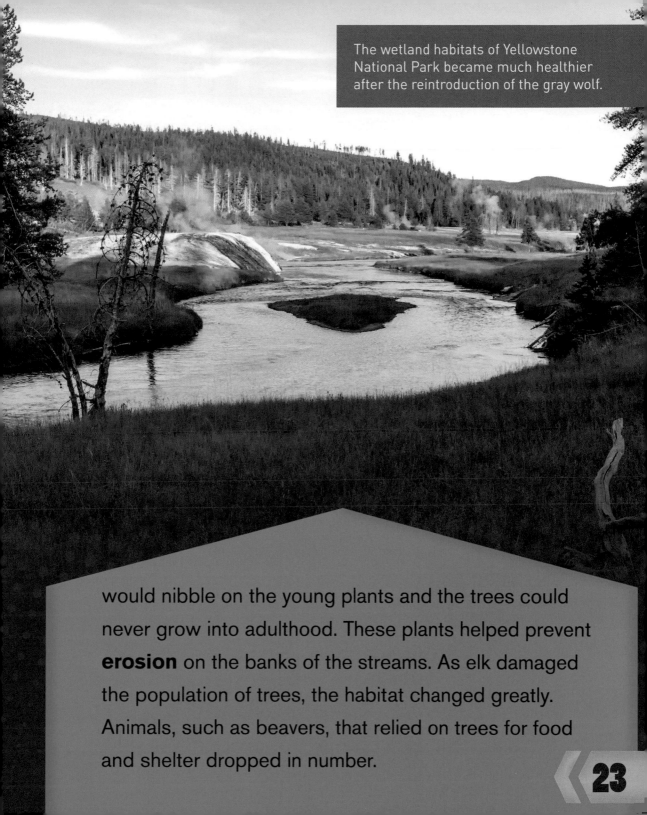

The wetland habitats of Yellowstone National Park became much healthier after the reintroduction of the gray wolf.

would nibble on the young plants and the trees could never grow into adulthood. These plants helped prevent **erosion** on the banks of the streams. As elk damaged the population of trees, the habitat changed greatly. Animals, such as beavers, that relied on trees for food and shelter dropped in number.

REINTRODUCTION

During the 1800s, when wolves were systematically hunted and killed, settlers weren't worried about the affect it would have on the ecosystem. They were only concerned with surviving. People now understand that losing any species, large or small, is dangerous to an entire ecosystem.

When wolves were reintroduced, the elk began to move around again. Before wolf reintroduction, the main

SCAVENGERS

You may think that reintroducing a top predator would mean there's less food for other predators. However, the new wolf population actually helped other meat-eaters such as bears and coyotes. Birds such as eagles and ravens also benefitted. That's because wolves tend to kill big animals and leave some of the meat behind. Scavengers clean up after wolf kills. The wolves do all the work, and the scavengers get to eat too!

Elk are very large animals. It takes a powerful hunter like the wolf to kill an elk. Coyotes are also Yellowstone predators, but they usually aren't strong enough to overtake an adult elk.

cause of death for Yellowstone elk was deep snow. Since wolves returned to Yellowstone, they have become the main cause of death for elk once again.

Since elk began to move again, the plants had time to recover and grow. This prevented erosion and provided shelter for smaller animals. Because these trees were back, the beaver population also increased.

A HEALTHY ECOSYSTEM

Scientists say that the healthiest ecosystems are those that have as many native plants and animals as possible. That's called biodiversity. The Yellowstone National Park ecosystem lost some of its biodiversity when the gray wolf was killed off.

The gray wolf's near extinction shows how much one animal can affect all the other animals in an ecosystem. As we learned with the Yellowstone trees, one animal can also affect the plant growth in an area and even nonliving aspects such as the erosion of riverbanks. After reintroducing the gray wolf, wildlife experts saw biodiversity recover within the Yellowstone ecosystem. If you visit Yellowstone National Park today, you'll see more aspens growing tall and more beavers building homes. Maybe you'll even spot the hero of this story—the gray wolf.

The gray wolf is important in the web of life that exists in Yellowstone National Park.

WHAT CAN YOU DO?

When animals are on the brink of extinction, saving them may seem like an impossible task. However, as the Yellowstone Wolf Project shows, these animals can bounce back and help balance their natural ecosystems. How can you help?

The Yellowstone Wolf Project accepts donations. With continued support, the project can keep up its efforts to save and understand the wolves of Yellowstone National Park.

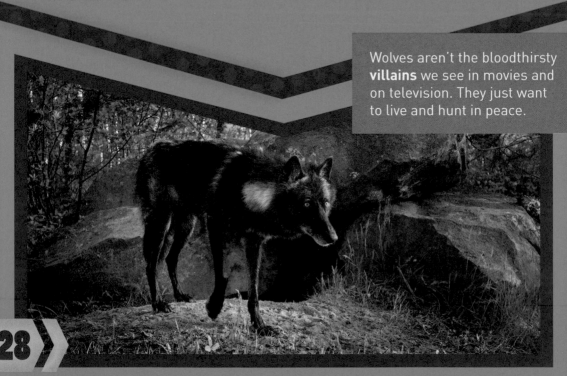

Wolves aren't the bloodthirsty **villains** we see in movies and on television. They just want to live and hunt in peace.

The best thing you can do is to educate others. Teach them what you've learned about wolves and their near extinction. Help others understand that wolves are not usually dangerous to people. In fact, there have only been two cases of a wolf killing a person in North America in the last 100 years. If people stop fearing the gray wolf, we can work even harder to protect it.

GRAY WOLVES THROUGH TIME

ca. 1877 People start poisoning dead bodies of hoofed animals so wolves would die.

U.S. Bureau of Biological Survey is established. **1885**

1906 U.S. Forest Service and the Bureau of Biological Survey begin working together to get rid of gray wolves living near cattle ranges.

The last gray wolf pack in Yellowstone National Park is killed. **1926**

1973 The Endangered Species Act is passed.

Congress approves money for a wolf restoration project. **1991**

1995 AND 1996 Wildlife experts release 31 gray wolves into Yellowstone National Park.

Wildlife experts release 10 more wolves into Yellowstone National Park. **1997**

2004 There are about 174 wolves in Yellowstone National Park.

There are 10 packs of wolves in Yellowstone National Park, 99 individuals in all. **2016**

GLOSSARY

conservationist: Someone who works to protect nature.

ecosystem: A natural community of living and nonliving things.

erosion: The wearing away of the earth's surface by wind or water.

descended: Born of a certain group or family.

fascinating: Very interesting.

hemisphere: One-half of Earth.

scavenger: An animal that eats what it can find, including waste and dead animals.

sponsor: To pay for the cost of an activity, organization, or event.

systematic: Using a careful system or method to do something.

tranquilize: To use a drug to cause an animal to become very relaxed and calm.

villain: Someone or something that is blamed for a problem.

INDEX

WEBSITES

Due to the changing nature of Internet links, PowerKids Press has developed an online list of websites related to the subject of this book. This site is updated regularly. Please use this link to access the list: www.powerkidslinks.com/bbe/wolf